Living Nature

FISH

Chrysalis Children's Books

The publishers wish to thank the following for permission to reproduce copyright material:

Oxford Scientific Films and individual copyright holders on the following pages: Fred Bavendam 6; Fredrik Ehrenstrom 24 top; Max Gibbs title page, contents page, 4, 5 bottom, 12 bottom, 17; Laurence Gould 16; Howard Hall 8 bottom; Pam & Willy Kemp 18/19; Breck P Kent/Animals Animals 10/11, 27 top; Rudie Kuiter 5 top, 13 bottom, 20 inset, 26; Zig Leszczynski/Animals Animals 7 centre and bottom, 14, 24 centre and bottom; Colin Milkins 9 bottom, Tsuneo Nakamura 25 top; J E Paling 7 top; Peter Parks 13 centre, 27 bottom; Robert Redden/ Animals Animals 8 top right; Kathy Tyrrell 20/21; P & W Ward 25 bottom; W Wisniewski/Okapia 11 top; Norbet Wu 15.

This edition first published in 2003 by
Chrysalis Children's Books
The Chrysalis Building, Bramley Rd,
London W10 6SP

Text copyright © Angela Royston
Photographs copyright © Oxford Scientific Films
and individual copyright holders
Format and illustrations © Chrysalis Books PLC

Printed in Hong Kong

ISBN 1 84138 629 4

British Library Cataloguing in Publication Data
CIP data for this book is available from the British Library

A Belitha Book

Editing: Serpentine Editorial
Series designer: Frances McKay
Consultant: Andrew Branson

Words in **bold** are in the glossary on page 30.

Title page: Clown loaches like this one live in the rivers of Indonesia.

Contents page: The purple sturgeon fish lives in the Red Sea.

Contents

Meet the fish

▶ The brightly coloured warty frog fish lives in tropical seas. It looks as strange as its name sounds.

The fish shown here are all extraordinary. Fish have strange shapes and are brightly coloured. They come from different parts of the world.

▶ The Hawaiian boxfish has small fins and a strange box-shaped body. It swims around the islands of Hawaii in the Pacific Ocean.

▼ The Red Indian fish has a long fin along its back like a Native American's head-dress. It lives off the coast of Australia.

All fish live in water – some in the sea, others in rivers and lakes. Many other animals, such as starfish, jellyfish and whales, live in water, too. Fish may not look alike, but they have some things in common that make them different from all other animals.

▶ The jigsaw trigger fish is also Australian. It lives on the world's largest **coral reef**, the Great Barrier Reef, off the east coast of Australia.

Types of fish

There are three main types of fish – jawless fish, sharks and rays, and bony fish. Jawless fish include lampreys and hagfish. They all have smooth, slimy skins.

Sharks and rays have rough, tough skins. Like jawless fish they have rubbery skeletons made of **cartilage**, not bone. Only the bony fish have hard bones and smooth **scales**.

◀ This trout has a river lamprey stuck to it. The lamprey's round mouth fixes on like a sucker while it feeds on the trout.

▲ A lamprey has no jaws. It uses its many tiny teeth to scrape away the flesh of its prey.

▶ The Moorish idol and the trout are both bony fish. There are four times as many kinds of bony fish as other fish.

◀ A spotted wobbegong shark lurks on the seabed. It does not look like a shark, but it has rough skin and a rubbery skeleton.

Breathing in water

All living things need to breathe in **oxygen**. Land animals, including humans, take oxygen from the air they breathe into their **lungs**.

▼ Fish take in oxygen through their gills. This reef shark has four gill slits behind its head, just in front of its fins.

◀ Lungfish live in lakes and marshes. They have gills and lungs. They use their gills under water. If the water dries up, they breathe in air through their lungs.

Most fish have gills instead of lungs. A fish swallows water through its mouth and pushes it out through its gills. As water passes over the gills, oxygen from the water passes into the fish's blood. At the same time **carbon dioxide** passes from the blood into the water.

▶ Bony fish have gill flaps that cover and protect their gills. The flap opens to let the water through.

Did you know?

Most fish open and shut their mouths to breathe, but some sharks just swim along with their mouths open.

▼ The side of this bony fish has been cut away to show the gills which are behind its eyes. The gills take in oxygen from the water as it flows over them.

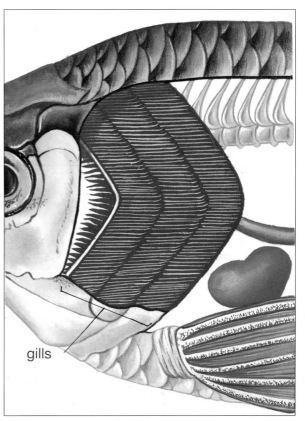

gills

Moving through water

A fish has very powerful **muscles** down the sides of its body. It uses them to move its tail from side to side to swim through the water. The blue-finned tunny can swim at over 60 kilometres an hour – seven times as fast as an Olympic swimmer.

▶ A bony fish has an extra **organ** – a swimbladder – inside its body. The swimbladder is filled with gas and allows the fish to move up and down in the water.

▼ Close up of the swimbladder in the fish below.

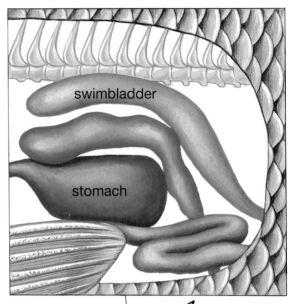

swimbladder

stomach

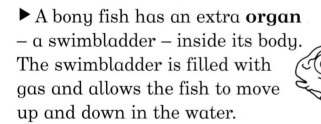

▶ Salmon can leap up and over a waterfall. They swim to the surface and flick their tails to glide through the air.

A bony fish has a swimbladder filled with gas to stop it sinking in the water. When the fish wants to rise, it lets more gas into the swimbladder. When it wants to sink deeper, it lets some gas out.

▼ Fish swim by moving their tails. The pickerell's long, thin shape helps it to swim fast through the water.

Fins

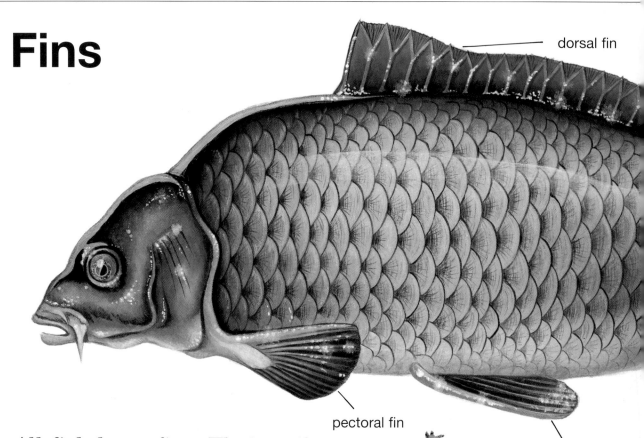

dorsal fin

pectoral fin

pelvic fin

All fish have fins. Their tail fin and muscles push them through the water. Their other fins help them to stop and steer, and keep them steady. If a fish wants to move slowly, it flaps its fins.

Some fish use their fins for other things too. Mudskippers sometimes leave the water to look for food. Then they use their fins like feet.

◄ A seahorse is a fish, although it doesn't look much like one. It has very small fins that move it slowly through the water.

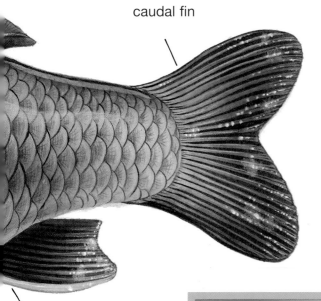

caudal fin

anal fin

▼ A flying gurnard has huge side fins. It uses them like wings when it leaps from the water and glides through the air.

◄ The lionfish has brightly coloured fins and poisonous spines. The large, waving fins warn other animals to stay away from the spines and not to try to eat it.

Seeing underwater

Most fish have big, bulging eyes on both sides of their heads. They can see all around and above and below at the same time. They look out for food and danger.

▶ A fish's eye is like a human eye, except that the **lens** is round and bulges through the **pupil**.

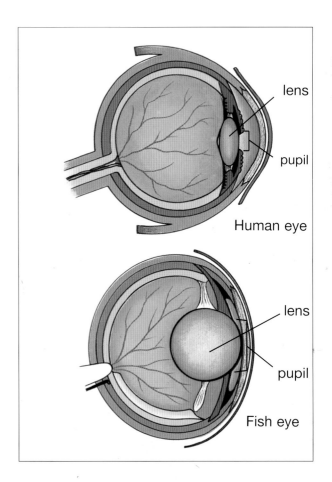

lens

pupil

Human eye

lens

pupil

Fish eye

▲ Mudskippers spend a lot of time sitting in shallow water or mud.

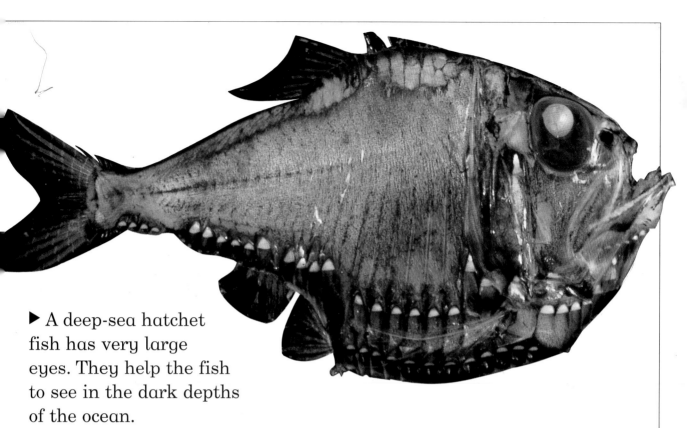

▶ A deep-sea hatchet fish has very large eyes. They help the fish to see in the dark depths of the ocean.

Mudskippers have eyes on top of their heads to see insects above the water. Some fish can see in very little light. The deeper they go in the sea the darker it becomes.

◀ The black sea dragon lives in total darkness in very deep sea. It makes its own light to attract fish into its huge, gaping jaws.

Making sounds

Sound travels better through water than it does through air. A fish does not need ears outside its head to hear underwater. Instead its ears are sealed inside its head, behind the eyes. Sounds travel through its body to the ears.

Fish can hear sounds many kilometres away. Many fish can make sounds, too. Some grind their teeth together, some rub their fins against their bodies. Many fish use their swimbladders to make a noise and to help them hear better.

▶ You cannot see a fish's ears because they are covered up inside its body.

▲ This catfish makes a noise with its swimbladder. Special muscles **vibrate** the swimbladder like a drum. The swimbladder also helps the fish to hear. Sound makes it vibrate like an **eardrum**.

▶ Loaches squeak like mice. They do this by blowing gas out of their swimbladders. You can make a similar noise by taking a blown-up balloon and pulling the mouth flat as you let the air out.

Did you know?

Many fish are very noisy eaters. Toad fish sound almost as loud as an underground train. Their noises warn other toad fish to keep away from their food.

Smelling and tasting

Smelling and tasting are more important to fish than to humans. A sharks has a very good sense of smell – more than half its brain is devoted to it. We taste with our tongues, but a fish has taste buds all around its head and in its mouth. It has **taste buds** on its body and front fins, too. Catfish and cod can taste with their whisker-like feelers.

◀ Sharks can smell blood up to two kilometres away. They quickly gather from all around when an animal is killed or wounded.

Did you know?

A salmon is born in a river then swims out to sea, but it always returns to the same river to breed. It finds the river by smell and by taste.

A special sense

Some fish have an extra, special sense. Along each side of their bodies they have a line, called the lateral line, which can detect the smallest movement in the water around them.

Did you know?

Dogfish can detect electricity. They find their prey from the tiny amounts of electricity which is given off by all moving animals.

► This perch has a lateral line on its side.

▼A shoal of sardines swims around a rock. Each fish changes direction and avoids the rock without bumping into any of the others.

The lateral line stops a fish swimming into rocks, or into the sides of a fish tank. It allows large groups, or shoals, of fish to swim close together. If the shoal is attacked, the fish swim off in all directions without colliding.

Feeding

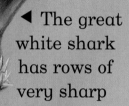

◄ The great white shark has rows of very sharp teeth. When one tooth falls out it is immediately replaced by another.

Some fish feed on plants, some hunt other fish and animals. Their teeth vary according to the kind of food they eat. Fish that eat meat have sharp teeth. Some bony fish have teeth on their tongues and in their throats, and also in their jaws.

◄ An angel fish feeds on hard coral. Its teeth have joined together into a sharp beak which cuts through the coral.

gill-rakers

Very often (but not always) big fish eat little fish, which feed on still smaller fish, which feed on plants. One of the very biggest fish, the basking shark, also feeds on plants. Its mouth has a special strainer called a gill-raker.

▲ A basking shark feeds on tiny plants and animals called plankton. It has a gill-raker in its mouth which strains the plankton from the water.

▶ Goldfish live in rivers and feed off the plants that grow on the bottom and sides of the river.

Defences

As well as finding food, fish try to avoid being eaten. Some fish, such as toad fish, stonefish, and weever fish, defend themselves with poisonous spines. The anemone fish defends itself by hiding in the poisonous tentacles of the sea anemone. Its slimy skin stops it being stung itself.

▲ The stonefish (at the top) has two defences. It has poisonous spines and it looks like a stone.

▲ The sargassum fish (in the centre) looks just like the seaweed it swims among.

◄ The anemone fish can swim safely among the stinging tentacles of the sea anemone.

Many fish defend themselves by looking like their surroundings. Fish that swim in the ocean are often dark on top, to look like the sea, and silvery below, to look like the sky.

▶ The leaf-fish looks like a dead leaf floating in the water. It is hard to make out its head and fins.

▲ When attacked, the spiny pufferfish swallows huge amounts of water to puff out its sharp, strong spines.

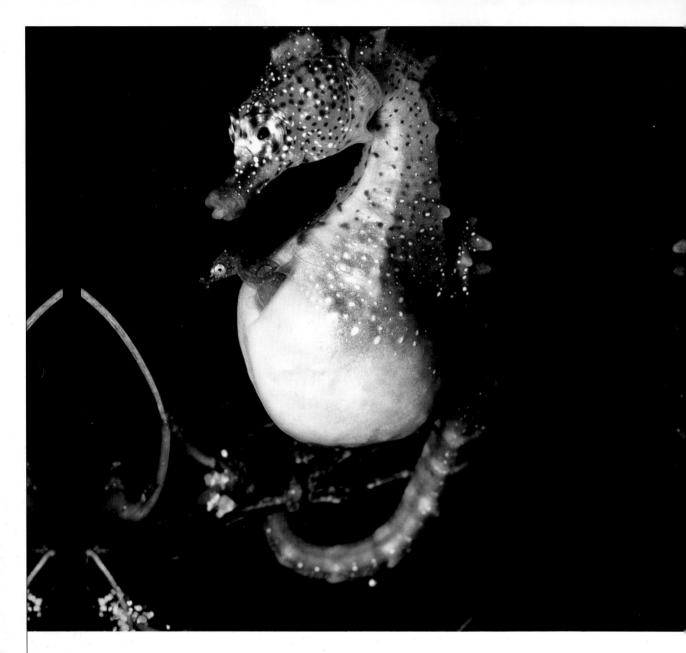

Creating young

It takes a male and a female fish to produce new fish. The female lays her eggs and the male **fertilizes** them with his sperm.

Most fish produce thousands of eggs. They leave them to float in the ocean, and many are eaten by other fish.

A few fish, such as seahorses, look after the eggs until they hatch. Sharks' eggs are fertilized inside the female and are born already hatched.

◀ The male seahorse looks after the fertilized eggs in a pouch on his belly.

▼ As the female brown trout lays her eggs, the male fertilizes the eggs with his sperm.

▲ A young rainbow trout hatching from its egg. The black spots are unhatched fish.

World of fish

Water covers nearly three-quarters of the Earth, and more than 20 000 different fish live in it. Some live in warm, tropical seas, especially around coral reefs.

But many fish prefer the cold water of the Arctic and Antarctic Oceans. Freshwater fish live in rivers, lakes and streams. Each fish is well suited to the place it lives.

Colourful fish
swimming
around coral
in the Red Sea.

Glossary

Carbon dioxide A gas that is carbon and oxygen combined together. It is one of the gases found in the air.

Cartilage A tough, rubbery substance that sharks and some other fish have instead of bones. Human ears are also made of cartilage.

Coral reef This looks like rock, but is the skeletons of countless tiny relatives of sea anemones.

Eardrum A thin skin stretched across the ear canal, which vibrates when sound waves reach it. The vibrations are passed through the ear to the brain.

Fertilizes When a male sperm joins with a female egg it fertilizes the egg. An egg must be fertilized before it can grow into a baby fish.

Fins Parts of a fish which stick out from its body and help it to move through the water.

Lens The part of the eye which focuses the light to give a clear picture.

Lungs Part of the body where oxygen from the air passes into the blood.

Muscle Meaty substance inside the body which makes the bones and other parts of the body move.

Organ A part of the body with a particular job to do. Animals have many kinds of organs, for example, a heart, stomach and eyes. Most bony fish also have a swimbladder.

Oxygen A gas which plants and animals need to stay alive. Oxygen is in air and in water.

Prey An animal hunted for food.

Pupil The black hole in the middle of the eye. Light goes through this into the eye.

Scales Small, flat plates that cover the skin and protect it.

Taste buds Special cells which react to chemicals and produce the sense of taste.

Vibrate Move backwards and forwards or up and down very fast.

Key facts

Largest fish The whale shark is the largest fish. It grows up to 18 metres long, nearly as long as two buses parked end to end.

Largest freshwater fish The beluga is a kind of sturgeon that lives in the Russian Federation. It grows up to 8.4 metres long, nearly as long as three cars. Its eggs provide the best caviar, a very expensive food.

Smallest fish The pygmy goby grows only about 12 mm long, about as long as your thumbnail.

Fastest fish A sailfish can reach 109 kilometres an hour. If a sailfish competed in the Olympics, it could swim nearly 12 lengths before the fastest human could swim one.

Most dangerous shark Great white sharks have attacked more humans than any other kind of shark, but tiger sharks are known for the fierceness with which they eat almost anything.

Most poisonous fish Stonefish probably have the most poisonous spines of any fish.

Most eggs laid The ocean sunfish lays up to 300 million eggs at a time. It lives in the sea and most of the eggs and young fish are eaten by other animals. Only one or two young sunfish survive to become adults.

Fewest eggs The stickleback lays only a few eggs. To protect the eggs, the male builds a nest of roots and leaves cemented into a tube with a special liquid. He then chases the female into the tube, where she lays the eggs. The male guards the fertilized eggs until they hatch.

Coldest fish Icefish live in the Antarctic Ocean where the water is often less than 0 degrees Centigrade. They have their own anti-freeze to stop their blood from freezing solid.

Earliest fish The first known fish were jawless fish called ostracoderms. They lived about 510 million years ago, and were covered in armour. The first bony fish were spiny sharks called acanthodians. They lived about 410 million years ago.

Index